cherrymoon
M E D I A

Copyright © 2018 Cherrymoon Media
All rights reserved.
www.cherrymoonmedia.com

ISBN-13: 978-0-9982190-3-5

FOUR VITAL QUES TIONS

FOR HIGH SCHOOL SENIORS

By Keen Babbage, Ed. D.

CONTENTS

INTRODUCTION

High school is an important time for learning, preparing, and planning. This book is designed to help guide you through your high school years and toward opportunities after high school.

This book is a gift for you. This book was written with you in mind. This book is for you. That's not all.

This book is all about you. For classes during your years in school and during free time you had, you have read many books. You have read biographies, novels, textbooks and many others. Some of those books became favorites of yours and you read them more than once. Other books were for a very specific purpose and when you finished it was put aside forever.

This book is all about you. This book is about what you have done so far in your life, what you are doing now in your life, the direction you are headed in your life, and how you can get the desired results you seek for your life. This book is yours to keep and re-read from time to time.

Think about your elementary, middle, and high school years. Recall some precise moments and experiences from each of those time periods. Where were you? What were you doing? What lessons were being learned? What skills were being acquired? What were your best achievements? What were the most serious challenges you faced and endured? What would you do differently if you had an opportunity to change something? Of course, you cannot change anything about the past, but lessons can and should be learned from your past.

Now, think about where you are today and what you are doing today. Are you where you expected to be when you used to imagine yourself at this moment?

Think about where you are going. Where will you be tomorrow, next year, two years from now, five years from now, 10 years from now, and much further? Are you confident that you are going where you have hoped, worked, and planned that you would be?

Think about how you are going to get to the place and activity that you want in your life. Are all of the plans made? Are all of the decisions made? What has to be done to carry out all of the plans and all of the decisions? What must you do to make the most of your next experience, your next adventure, your next responsibility, your next endeavor? What can be done and what must be done for the parts of your life that are in the longer-term future, in addition to those parts that will be completed in the next several years?

You and I have not met, but in some very real ways we do know each other. You have been in school for many years from kindergarten through high school. I have worked in middle schools and in high schools for 34 years. You have known many teachers and school administrators. I have taught many students. We have had some similar experiences.

Plus, I vividly recall my years during kindergarten through high school. Having reflected upon those years for over four decades, it is my conclusion that as you go through high school there are four vital questions that you need to ask, think about, and answer. It is my hope that you will benefit from this book, which is designed to guide you through meaningful, personal, important consideration of those four vital questions as they apply to you.

This book is all about you. This book is all for you. In fact, you are the co-author of this book. Congratulations, in addition to the work you are doing to become a high school graduate, you are becoming the co-author of a book! There will be thinking for you to do as you read this book and there will be writing for you to do. Does that sound similar to work you have done in school? Yes, it does, so it will build upon and apply those school experiences. That is part of the idea that we must continue to learn throughout life and continue to learn about life.

There will be times in this book when I, as the author, enter into a conversation with you. Sentences, paragraphs, questions, and ideas will be addressed to you. As you read those words, know that any reference to you is to you, the reader. That is my attempt to make this conversation between author and reader/co-author as personal as possible.

There will be many other times in this book when you, as the co-author, enter into a conversation with yourself. In those parts of the book, you are not addressed as you; rather, the pronoun is "I" which enables you to interact directly with yourself, your thoughts, your ideas, your reflections, your hopes, and your plans.

Participate eagerly and genuinely in both of those types of conversations. Think clearly, accurately, honestly, and boldly. Listen closely.

There are some guidelines to follow. First, students in my classroom have always been told that everything said or done there must be "G-rated, legal and ethical." Those are honorable standards to follow in a classroom, elsewhere, and when answering the four vital questions of this book.

Second, students of mine have also been told to live up to this standard: "Results, not excuses." Again, that idea applies to academic work done for school and to other endeavors, including serious reflection upon the four vital questions facing each emerging high school graduate.

Third, I have advised and encouraged students for many years to "read, read more, keep reading." As you read this book, also "think, think more, keep thinking." Actively read this book. React to this book.

Write your parts of the book, making the book even more uniquely about you and for you. Then take the determined, ethical, wise actions which will enable you to live a meaningful life of purpose, honor, integrity, persistence, determination, goodness, joy, and achievements, now and always.

-Keen Babbage, Ed. D.
Lexington, Kentucky
2018

THE FOUR VITAL QUESTIONS

It is now. It is always now. There is no other time except now. Or is there? We can think about yesterday in particular and about the past in general. We can intellectually revisit the past. It is very important to think about yesterday, to reflect upon yesterday, and to understand yesterday. We can analyze and learn from yesterday.

We can regret yesterday. We can celebrate yesterday. We cannot relive yesterday, but we can live better today through having a deep understanding of our past. We live now and now is the only time we can live, yet part of living well now includes knowing our past fully.

Although we cannot live in the future, we can build a solid foundation for that future. We can prepare for that future, we can train ourselves for that future, we can get the necessary education our desired future requires, we can gain the skills our future needs, and we can take actions today which help direct us to the future we envision.

Still, life occurs now and the life we plan for is determined largely by the life we live now. As you continue reading, remember that "I" in each of these questions refers to you, as do most other "I" references in this book. This book is about you. It is time for you to begin an important conversation with yourself.

Question One is – where have I been? That question is a sincere welcome to know my past, my successes, my failures, my lessons learned, my opportunities fully embraced, my opportunities missed, and to gain new insights based on new reflection. I cannot return to the past, but I can reflect upon my past in search of guidance for my present and for my future.

Question Two is – where am I now? I am here. I am always here. I can be no place except here. No matter where I am, that place is defined as here. I can think of other places I have been. I can make plans to be in other places at other times. I can be at only one place at one time. Here is where I always am.

There is more to "where am I now?" than to identify the physical location I occupy at this moment. I can think this way: where am I in terms of my education, my maturity, my relationships, my plans, my dreams, my hopes, my problems, and my responsibilities? For a person my age, am I where I should be now in these important aspects of life?

I live right now and right here. There is no other way to live, no other time to live, and no other place to live. Here and now do not confuse me or surprise me; rather, they present challenges and opportunities. Will I make the most of here and now? How will I make the most of here and now? Will I maximize the potential goodness of here and now, or will I waste it?

There is a liberation which comes from knowing that I get to answer those questions rather than have the answers forced upon me. Yet there is a reality which insists that there are some limitations, some restrictions, some boundaries that here and now use to constrain me, to guide me, to manage me.

Perhaps those boundaries are for my safety and for my protection. Perhaps some of those boundaries are limitations that I need to overcome. There is nothing easy about analyzing here and now, yet there is a vital need to do that analysis continually.

Question Three is – where am I going? I am going to a new here, but where and what is that new here? It may be the same overall location where I am today, but something about the place changes or I change how I interact with the same place. Perhaps I will have a new experience in the same place.

I may be moving to a new location and that will bring some adjustments. Will the new here and now be what I planned for, intended, designed, hoped for, worked for, and committed to, or will factors beyond my control impact or even determine who and what I become as I have new experiences?

My initial thought about question three may be that the answer, at least in part, has been reached already. I know where I am going next in my life. Yet, there is still room for further consideration of how that decision of where I am going will be implemented and of changes that may need to be made in that implementation as it progresses. Where I am going is an emerging work-in-progress that is open to improvement.

The answer to question three should never be, "Oh, you know, wherever life takes me. I mean, things will just happen the way they happen." Such lethargic thinking and fatalistic living are unacceptable to the spirit and inherent power of the four vital questions to think about as I work to graduate from high school.

Question Four is – how will I get there? Actions must be planned, and actions must be taken to get me from where I am now to where I am going. I will get there by taking very specific, sensible, smart, purposeful actions. I will not get there by waiting for there to come to me. I must go to there.

These questions and contemplations may seem to me at first glance to be somewhat abstract, rather deep, and quite profound. That is true, but it is not all of the truth. Those descriptions are only a few of the colors which combine to create the complete portrait of fully knowing my genuinely personal answers to the four vital questions I need to ask and answer as I work to graduate from high school.

Your meaningful conversation with yourself has begun. You are beginning to think about the four vital questions to answer as you work to graduate from high school: Where have I been? Where am I now? Where am I going? How will I get there? This book is designed to lead you, the reader, on a tour of where you have been and of where you are while also guiding you to where you are going and how you will get there.

There will be no automatic, superficial, or useless answers. These questions are not part of a test which will be graded. These questions are part of an adventure which needs to be identified, acknowledged, evaluated, designed, improved, embraced, implemented, and lived, fully lived.

As you read this book and as you identify your

answers to the four vital questions, be honest, really honest. Here's an example: you took a Physics class in high school and the topic just made no sense to you. You made an effort for a month or two, but then decided that your only goal for the class was to avoid failing it. You rarely studied, and you never paid full attention in class. You barely avoided failing the class.

Now, you realize that there were ways that you could have done much better in the Physics class. There were after school study sessions you could have attended. There were before school help sessions that the teacher provided, but you decided to just talk with friends during those times instead of attending the help sessions. If you regret not doing all you could have done to learn more in Physics and to have done better in that class than barely getting by with a D- grade, admit that and indicate what you now realize about that situation and about similar situations. Give yourself the gift of applying that new insight.

Perhaps you were an absolute scholar in Physics, so that example does not apply to you. Think of other situations when you could have made more effort, could have made a better effort, or might have pursued a high-quality opportunity that for some reason you rejected. Learn from that reflection and analysis.

Be equally honest about your successes, achievements and improvements. You needed to earn money one summer, so you started your own yard service business. You cut the grass for many neighbors and you did additional yard work. Acknowledge your effort, your determination, and your success. Perhaps you started doing some babysitting, and neighbors you worked for recommended you to friends of theirs. Give yourself credit for that good work.

Where have you been? Where are you now? Where are you going? How will you get there? Let's find out. In finding out the answers to those questions, you'll earn the priceless gifts of insight, knowledge, wisdom, possibilities, plans, direction, action, and results.

WHERE HAVE I BEEN?

Where you have been does include geography and locations, but also includes experiences and ideas, plus people and relationships. It is time to think, think more, keep thinking, and become the co-author of this book. Ready, set, think, write!

Think of different locations you have visited, the impact those sites had on you, and the various experiences you had there. Those locations may be in one city or may include various cities. The emphasis is not on miles journeyed; rather, it's on experiences, on insights gained, on lessons learned, on mistakes made, on successes achieved, on people known, and on some moments permanently etched into your memory.

As you think and as you prepare to write, consider the following thoughts expressed by a person who is graduating from high school now, just as you are or soon will. She was asked to reflect on where she had been during the time between birth and graduation from high school.

I've been several places. My family moved a few times. We have been in this city for nine years, but before that we lived in two other cities. I think of this place as home because my most important memories and experiences are from here.

Where have I been? Well, like a lot of us when we are children, I have been through stages when I had these pretty wild ideas of what I would be when I grew up. I really wanted to be a pilot. When my brother, sister, and I would play outside, whenever I saw a plane I would stop whatever I was doing and just stare. The whole idea of a machine flying like that amazed me.

Then I got interested in carpentry. When my family moved to this city we bought a house that needed a lot of work. My family did almost all of that work. I was too young to help much with the actual construction part of the job, but I sure was curious about everything that was going on and I helped in any way that a nine-year-old could. I was so amazed at how cool the house looked when we were finished with all the renovation work.

Then in middle school I decided I wanted to write books for children and teenagers. I always read a lot of books. An author visited my middle school. I had read one of her books. I was so excited that she signed my copy of her book. The book was all about animals. I really love animals, so I wondered if I should become a veterinarian, but I kept thinking that I would rather be an author. Then in high school that changed.

In high school, I had a lot of really interesting classes and some great teachers. One day I would be fascinated with science experiments, and the next day I would concentrate on something from U.S. History. I was in the marching band and that meant a lot to me. Then what really got my attention in high school was a music class I took when I was a sophomore. My music teacher kept telling us that there was a lot of creativity in music, but that there was also a lot of math and science in music. I had never heard that before, but I realized that it really is true.

Since I already liked music a lot, I started paying much more attention in math class and in science class to understand those subjects better and to see how they connected to music. The more I looked for connections, the more I found what connected math and science and music. That's when I decided I wanted to concentrate on math and on music. I took all of those high school classes that I could. I loved it. I really loved it.

I worked really hard in high school. Marching band took a lot of time. I had classes to study for, and I knew that it was important to make good grades. I had a job each summer, and I kept working part-time during the school year when I was a junior and a senior, but I could not work at my part-time job very much during the marching band seasons.

I have learned a lot during these 18 years. From wanting to be a pilot to all those other ideas I had, to now wanting to be a high school band director, I can see how I finally found what I really want to become; well, at least what I think I want to become based on what I know now.

I know people who have graduated from high school, and when they graduated they thought they knew what they wanted to do and then changed their mind and did something different. Today, I really think that I want to become a high school band director. Could that change? Sure, and if another idea comes along which leads me in another direction for the right reasons, that would be fine.

So far, when I think of where I have been, most of the memories are good, but there have been some difficulties. My mother had an accident a few years ago and broke her right leg. For a few months she could not do much, but everyone in the family helped her and we did what she could not do at home for her. That's when I learned to cook. I am no great chef, but I can fix a good meal. It also made me realize how much my mother means to me. I appreciate her more than ever.

Then there was the time my father's company got bought by some other company. The new owner reduced the number of employees, and my father lost his job. Helping him find his next job became a project for our entire family. Until he found his new full-time job, he had three part-time jobs and worked about 16 hours each day, 6 or 7 days each week just to make enough for us to get by. Plus, my mother kept working at her job, but that company had bad times and her hours were reduced, so she had to get a second part-time job, too. I really respected their determination to keep making enough money for our family.

Those were really tough times. We cut everything out of our family budget that we could. I remember hearing my parents talk about whether we should pay the electric bill or the water bill. They talked about whether they should pay the mortgage or the car payment. They decided to sell one of our two cars. Now, Dad's new job is even better than his old job was, and Mom's company eventually was able to give her more hours, but it was not easy during those times when money was scarce. I developed a new respect for my parents.

I get along well with my brother and my sister, but when we were young we had our disagreements. Now all of that seems pretty childish. We give each other lots of encouragement and help now. It's better that way. I want to have a family of my own someday, but I think it will be five or 10 years from now before that can start to happen.

There was one time when I was 12 and I was riding on my bicycle. I had a terrible accident. My collar bone broke. When I was 14, I had to get glasses. When I was 16, I got my driver's license. The truth is that I did not pass the driving test the first time. I was so embarrassed. I almost decided to give up. If cars were going to drive themselves someday, why would I need a license? Well, I pulled myself together and practiced a lot. I took the test a second time and made a perfect score. That taught me to never give up.

Two of my grandparents are still alive. They live in the same town where I live. I visit them often and I ask them a lot of questions. It means a lot to me to know about our family history. Plus, they are really smart people. They have learned a lot during their lives, and I want to know everything they know. They taught *me some important lessons about being honest, working hard, and being polite.*

My other two grandparents died when I was in elementary school. I remember them pretty well. I also remember how much I cried when they died. My grandfather died when I was in third grade, and my grandmother died when I was in fifth grade. I always visited them in the summer when I was really young. They lived on a farm. They let me feed the animals and ride on a horse. Those were great times.

So, where have I been? I have been in several different schools, a few different towns, and through a variety of interests about what I wanted to be when I grew up. I have had responsibilities. I have made mistakes and learned from them. I hate to admit it, but I once stole five dollars from my brother. He had made me mad, so I was going to get even with him.

My parents made me return the five dollars and then they made me earn five more dollars to give to my brother. Plus, I had to wash the supper dishes for a month, and I had to do some volunteer work at a local food bank. All of that because as a 10-year-old I stole five dollars from my brother. My parents told me that it is wrong to steal, and I sure did learn that lesson. My parents were right about that. The older I get the more I realize that my parents are right about a lot of things. They seem to get smarter as I get older. Interesting how that works, isn't it?

I'm sure there are more memories and experiences I could include, but I think the most important ones have been mentioned. I am very thankful for where I have been. The good times have been great, and the tough times have been endured. These 18 years are a solid foundation.

Now it is your turn. Where have you been? You may prefer to write in the space provided below, to use other paper to write your ideas on, to use an electronic device, or to use several writing methods. That choice is yours. Take a few moments before you write anything so you can think deeply and reflect thoroughly on the first of the four vital questions to answer as you work to graduate from high school: "Where have I been?"

———

Now, take a few minutes and read what you wrote. As you read those words, think of anything else that now comes to mind which originally you did not recall or think was important, but now you realize that you need to include it. Part of the reader and co-author-friendly design of this book is that there is no time limit for the parts that you write, and there is no maximum number of words you may write. Think, think more, keep thinking.

What additional thoughts now come to mind about the question: "Where have I been?"

———

You are now officially the co-author of a book about you. There is more to read and there is more to write. There is more to think about and more to learn. We are now ready to move to the second vital question for you to answer as you work to graduate from high school. "Where am I now?"

WHERE AM I NOW?

Right here, right now, where am I? I am becoming a high school graduate. That says a lot about where I am now in terms of my education, in terms of my age, in terms of my human growth and development, and in regard to the overall sequence of steps which I have taken between birth and now.

Let's look further and deeper. Where am I now in terms of ideas, understandings, and feelings? What do I support? What do I oppose? Where am I now regarding what I believe in, what I care about, what I wonder about, what I know about life, what I would like to know about life, and other aspects of what makes me the person that I am right here, right now?

(Some topics are provided to get your thoughts started and then some room is available for your additional ideas.)

Some people who are really important to me, and why they are so important to me...

Some things I wonder about and would like to know more about...

Some ideas I really strongly support, and why I support them...

———

Some ideas I really strongly oppose, and why I oppose them...

———

Some good things that go on in our country that I would like to get involved in and do something about, and why those things matter to me...

———

*Some things that go on in our country that really
bother me, concern me, and I hope I can help
change...*

Some things in life that I understand well and that I am certain about...

———

*Some things in life that I do not understand, but
hope that someday I will figure out...*

———

Some of the strongest feelings I have are...

_____

I am old enough to vote now or soon will be. For a candidate to get my vote, the candidate would have to convince me that...

———

Something I have changed my mind on through the years, and why I changed my mind...

———

Something I believe in very deeply...

———

Something that is on my mind a lot...

———

Important responsibilities I have now...

———

*I have some very good friends. The type of people I
become friends with are people who...*

———

*Something I am very sure about and have been
sure about for a long time...*

———

Something I am not so sure about...

———

Something I would like to get better at...

———

Something I would like to learn how to do...

---

*Something I am good at now that I was not good
at before…*

Something else I have made progress on...

___

A bad habit I have that I need to correct...

———

What other ideas, questions, experiences, thoughts, feelings, hopes, lessons learned, mistakes made, successes gained, and more complete my answer to the question: "Where am I now?"

———

Way to go. You put a lot of thought into exploring the second of the four vital questions. Perhaps your thinking brought some new ideas to mind. That thinking may have confirmed what you already knew, but it may also have provided you with some new insight. Plus, your thinking may have brought some new topics to think about, some new goals, some new ideas, and some new possibilities.

You have seriously and thoroughly considered "Where have I been?" and "Where am I now?" It is time to apply all of those thoughts and to move to the third vital question to answer as you work to graduate from high school: "Where am I going?"

WHERE AM I GOING?

At first glance, the question "Where am I going?" seems to suggest that identifying a certain location or a few locations would be the type of answer which is expected. That makes sense and that is part of the answer, but there is more.

"Where am I going?" also includes having an understanding of why I am going where I am going. Is where I am going the best option for me, or is it just the only option available now? Is where I am going the result of a serious evaluation of many possibilities, or is it just what, well, you know, kind of, sort of seems to be worth a try since nothing else came up?

Is where I am going next a step toward where I eventually intend to be, and, if so, how will I make sure that one step leads to the next desired step? How many steps will there be until I reach the ultimate goal? How will I make sure that each step is completed successfully, that each next step is available to me, and that I am fully ready for each next step?

"Where am I going?" includes options for more education, for specific job training, for military service, for immediate employment, and for other possibilities; however, there is more to "where I am going?" than those experiences. What else could there be?

Where I am going includes an evaluation and awareness of the direction I am going in terms of essential and honorable human characteristics such as honesty, acceptance of responsibility, doing what is right, proper behavior, concern for other people, manners, work ethic, and people skills. Am I going in the right direction in terms of those factors?

Take some time now to thoroughly explore question three: "Where am I going?" Be aware that on the day you graduate from high school, it is likely that some people will ask you, "What are you going to be doing now that you are a high school graduate?" They expect to hear about your plans for more education such as a two-year degree or a four-year degree from college; for specific job training experience that you will have through vocational, technical, or trade school education; for entering the military; for entering the workforce; or for other endeavors such as a combination of work part-time, an internship, doing volunteer work part-time, and/or taking a class or two online to see what interests you.

Let's list those options below with this plan: for the one which applies to you, explain why that is where you are going and for the other options which do not apply to you, explain why each of those is not where you are going.

A two-year college degree

———

A four-year college degree

———

Vocational, technical, or trade school

———

The military

The workforce

Other endeavors

The question "Where am I going?" asks more than where am I going to be tomorrow or in a few weeks or months. Where I am going now will impact where I go after that and in years or decades to come.

If I am going to college for a two-year or four-year degree, where I am going impacts the next two years or four years and impacts what I will do after those years once I have earned the degree.

The same is true if I am going to a vocational, technical, or trade school program. Perhaps this will be full-time study, or perhaps this will be a combination of study and working at a job, but either way it impacts the years during which I am in that program and what I will do once I have completed the requirements of the program.

If I am going into the military, do I envision doing that for a few years to complete an initial obligation, or do I see myself establishing a long-term career in the military?

If I am entering the workforce, is that going to be a job which is full-time from the start, is it part-time with hopes to move to full-time, or is it more than one job at different places?

If my plan is for other endeavors, how long do I expect that to continue, and what will those endeavors lead me to?

Select the option which applies to you and think about "where am I going?" in terms of a longer time frame than tomorrow, the next few weeks, or the next few months. Based on where you are going soon, where could that lead you for some or many years to come? Space is provided for you to write your thoughts as you continue to apply and develop your skills as the co-author of this book.

My option and the long-term results and
opportunities it can lead me to...

———

There is another category to consider in the overall topic of "where am I going?" Where are you going in terms of the kind of person you are becoming? Earlier in this book, as you answered vital questions one and two you thought about "where have I been?" and "where am I now?" Perhaps those considerations enabled you to notice some very important growth and progress you have made as a person. Perhaps those considerations also enabled you to identify some areas in your life which you would like to improve and to enhance. Let's consider where you are going as it relates to the person you hope to become.

No doubt, some of your characteristics and traits will not change much over time. For example, if you are already dedicated to hard work, it is important to maintain that dedication to a great work ethic. Yet just as you have changed some in appearance over the years – sure, you still have the charming smile you had as a child, but some features of your appearance have changed over the years, and in the decades to come there will be more physical changes – there can be some very intentional changes within your heart and your mind over the years as you identify ways to become an even better person. Think about the insights and the thoughts of one high school graduate who had the following ideas about the question: "Where am I going?"

Where am I going? I am going to college, and I plan on becoming an expert in information technology. My dream would be to create my own start-up company someday. But, in addition to that and just as important as that, maybe more important than that, I want to become more and more like my parents and my grandparents. They are such great people. I want to be an expert in my career, but I also want to be an expert in everything else that really matters in life. Here's what I mean.

My mother is the most caring person I know. She is so kind and thoughtful. She always thinks of what she can do for other people. She also works really hard. She is a fantastic cook. I mean, the meals she serves us are better than any restaurant. A few years ago, a friend of hers told her that she should open a restaurant. Instead of doing that, my mother opened a catering company. She has been so successful, it is amazing.

During my junior and senior years of high school, I worked for my mother on the weekends and in the summer. I loved working with her. I learned a lot about business and about food. I also got more serious about school just because I realized that the people who accomplish the most are the people who know and work a lot. I really want to become more and more like my mother in so many ways.

I also have learned a lot from my father. He is the manager of a car repair shop. He knows everything there is to know about cars. I have spent some time at the shop he manages. He has taught me so much about how a car works. He said I could save a lot of money if I knew how to do some basic maintenance of a car myself. He's right. Plus, I got to see how he interacted with customers. His shop is known for great customer service. It reminded me that treating people the right way is what we should do. Plus, it pays off in many ways.

My grandparents are wonderful people. I have spent time with all of them. My mother's parents live fairly close to us and my father's parents live further away, but I have gotten to know all of them. What I have noticed is how completely dedicated to each other they are. My parents are devoted to each other, too, but there is something about people who have been married to each other for 40 or 50 years and have always been really in love with each other. I would like to have that experience in my life when the time is right.

I am fortunate to know my grandparents so well. That did not happen for some of my friends because their grandparents live so far away or are no longer living. I have also met some wonderful people who are the age of my grandparents through volunteer work I did for a senior citizens' center. It was part of a service project we did with a club I was in during high school. There are ways to get to know people from an older generation, and the truth is they have learned a lot about life through their experiences. Whether it is your grandparents or other older people you get to know, they can give you some ideas and advice about where you are going.

So, when I think of where I am going, I think of my next step in education. My goal is to become an expert in information technology, so I am going to school for that in a few months. I also think about where I am going as a person. I want to continue to work hard. I also want to become more skilled in how I work with other people. I want to completely follow the examples my parents have set in people skills. Plus, I want to get the wisdom and the joy that my grandparents have.

I know there will be challenges and difficulties. My parents and my grandparents have told me about tough times they faced and managed to get through. Still, despite the certainty of challenges and difficulties that I will face, I see so much that interests me and so much that can be done. I am excited about where I am going, and I can't wait to start going there.

Now it is time for you, the co-author of this book, to do some more writing. Think about where you are going as it relates to the type of person you are now, who you intend to be in the next few years, and since there is always room for personal improvement and growth in every person, think also of the type of person you intend to become as you advance through your adult years.

Our adventure in thinking, in writing, in answering these vital questions continues. Having just thought about "where am I going?" your attention now turns to the fourth question: "How will I get there?"

HOW WILL I GET THERE?

Let's eliminate some ways which certainly will not get you there. It will not be handed to you. It will not just somehow appear one of these days. It will not be achieved by doing zero work. It will not be given to you just because you think you deserve it or think life owes you some favors. You will not arrive there through luck or by winning the lottery. You will not get there by wishing that there would come to you.

With those reminders about what is unrealistic having been acknowledged and renewed in your memory, let's concentrate now on what is realistic. The question is "how will I get there?" What is the answer? Are there several different answers which need to be evaluated? Are there several answers which can work together to create one big answer? Are there many parts to the answer? How is the answer found? How have other people figured out the answer to the fourth vital question? Can I learn something from those people?

For the rest of this chapter, you will do all of the work. You are ready to do all of the work, and it is important that you lead the way on this part of the book that you are co-authoring. For almost all of this chapter, you move from being the co-author to the author, so you are in charge, and you determine the result. You can do this and will benefit from doing this.

Part of the work you will do for this chapter as you answer, "how will I get there?" involves doing some serious research. You are going to talk to people so you can gain from their experience, their lessons learned, their insights, their mistakes made, their achievements attained, and their guidance.

One way to succeed in doing something is to get advice from people who have succeeded in doing the same thing. What do they know, what have they learned, what would they do differently, and what would they not change?

Also, there can be useful advice from people who did not succeed, or who did not succeed as much as they had hoped, in their attempt to do what you intend to do. What obstacles can they advise you about? What mistakes did they make which they now realize and can caution you about? Did they have some success, but now realize how they could have been more successful?

Step one is for you to have five in-depth discussions. These will be with five different people. First, talk with someone who is just a year or two years older than you are and who has been doing what you are going to do next, but has not finished it. Second, talk with someone who has completed recently what you are going to do next.

Third, talk with people who are twice your age, three times your age, four times your age. The specific questions you ask these three people may be different from the questions you asked the first two people, but seek advice, seek counsel, seek to know their life lessons learned. Ask them if they had the years right after high school graduation to do over again, what would they do differently and what would they not change at all.

Ask everyone you talk with a lot of why questions, how questions, when questions, what questions, and ask them to tell you if there were any questions you should have asked, but that you did not ask so those questions can be added to the discussions.

A format is provided so you can write the content of the discussions which are the first step in the research you are doing. Here's the format which, of course, you may alter. Just be sure that you get the type of information, insights and advice which this format emphasizes. This reading and writing is personal. This is all about you. This is of, by, and for you.

A conversation with someone who is just a year or two older than I am...

First Question:

Answer:

Second Question:

Answer:

Third Question:

Answer:

Fourth Question:

Answer:

Fifth Question:

Answer:

A conversation with someone who has recently completed what I am going to be doing next...

———

First Question:

Answer:

Second Question:

Answer:

Third Question:

Answer:

Fourth Question:

Answer:

Fifth Question:

Answer:

A conversation with someone who is about twice my age...

First Question:

Answer:

Second Question:

Answer:

Third Question:

Answer:

Fourth Question:

Answer:

Fifth Question:

Answer:

A conversation with someone who is about three times my age...

First Question:

Answer:

Second Question:

Answer:

Third Question:

Answer:

Fourth Question:

Answer:

Fifth Question:

Answer:

A conversation with someone who is about four times my age...

———

First Question:

Answer:

Second Question:

Answer:

Third Question:

Answer:

Fourth Question:

Answer:

Fifth Question:

Answer:

You have heard some important ideas, advice, and guidance. You have learned about mistakes made and mistakes learned from. You have learned about achievements and successes. You have learned what people would do if they had a decision to make over again or an action to take over again. You have heard from several different people.

You are ready for step two of this research project. Think about what you heard from everyone you talked to. What are the overall conclusions you can reach based on this research you have done? Put everything you asked people and everything the people said into conclusions which can help guide you. Write (a) your summary of the research, (b) your analysis of the research, and (c) your list of specific ways that you can apply what you have been told by the people you talked with for this research adventure.

It is hoped that you saw the research project as an adventure in learning and experienced it as an adventure in learning. It is also hoped that you remember for many years to come that getting advice, insights, and wise counsel from other people can be part of future decision making you do when, at times in your adult years, you find it will be useful to ask yourself anew the four vital questions you are asking yourself now.

Summary

Analysis

Specific actions I can take

———

Your research adds much very important content to this book which you are the accomplished co-author of. Put that research to good use now and in years to come. Occasionally re-read this book, including the writing you did. Continue to do the type of research you did to answer question four, especially as you face certain pivotal moments or very significant decisions in your life.

Let's pay some attention to an intellectual experience which very likely was part of your research. As you listened to the answers people gave to the questions you asked, there were probably times when you said to yourself, "Wow, I never thought of that" or "Yeah, that makes sense. I had never thought of it that way." Getting the perspective and the wise advice of other people addresses the realities that no one person thinks of everything and that no one person knows everything.

It is likely that there were times when you heard from people as they explained the impact of a decision they made or an action they took. They went on to explain how one action led to another action which led to later actions. That helped you realize the importance of fully thinking through a decision in terms not only of the immediate impact of a decision, but also in terms of how that decision can lead to future decisions or future consequences, some of which are good, yet some of which could be bad.

Remember this reality: actions and decisions made today lead to or impact actions in the future. Thinking through the immediate impact of a decision or of an action is essential. It is also essential to realize and to consider the long-term impact of decision making and of taking the best action.

EPILOGUE: FROM POTENTIAL TO REALITY

This book concludes with a personal letter from the author of the book to the co-author/reader of the book.

You know where you have been, where you are now, where you are going, and how you will get there. That knowledge is crucial, precious, and the foundation for a magnificent call to action. You had some of that knowledge before you read this book. You have added to your knowledge by reading this book and by co-authoring this book.

Because of the knowledge that you have, I am confident that you will work to achieve fully what you are capable of. I am confident that you are dedicating yourself to the idea that your potential – what you are capable of achieving, of being, and of becoming – can and will become reality. The combination of that bold thought and that determined approach avoids later regret over what might have been.

Because of experiences you have had, education you have obtained, and the knowledge you have, I am confident that you are eager and ready to achieve much, to set an example, to have great career success, and to live a very good life.

I am confident that you will live a high-quality life and that you will make a difference for good for other people.

I am confident that you will work to reach your potential for goodness, for achievement, for honor, for integrity, for joy, for persistence, for overcoming obstacles, for kindness, plus for G-rated, ethical, legal results in all that you do.

May you never be satisfied with good enough. May you seek much more than good enough. May you always strive to be your best. May you commit to this standard: results, not excuses.

I am confident that your life will always give a high priority to making on-going progress as you seek and find ways to grow as a person throughout all the years of your life. Progress results when a flame is ignited in the hearts and minds of those who refuse to accept today as the ultimate of human potential. Make that progress happen. Be that progress. Throughout your life and by your example, show yourself and show others how to confidently and intentionally advance from potential to reality.

You know where you have been, you know where you are now, you know where you are going, and you know how you will get there. Go for it.

ABOUT THE AUTHOR

Keen Babbage, Ed. D., retired from a 27-year career in public education in 2016. He had been a middle school teacher, a middle school assistant principal, and a high school teacher. Earlier and later in his career, he worked for seven years at three private schools. He has also worked in advertising/marketing for eight years at three large companies.

He has written 20 books about education with emphasis on two areas: teaching, and school leadership/management. He has written three additional books: *Life Lessons from Cancer* (co-authored by Laura Babbage); *Life Lessons from a Dog Named Rudy*; and *Take More Naps*. He lives in Lexington, Kentucky.

www.ingramcontent.com/pod-product-compliance
Lightning Source LLC
Chambersburg PA
CBHW022011090426
42741CB00007B/989